UNDATED 12 MONTH WEEKLY PLANNER

WITH AFFIRMATIONS

Susan McKenzie

Notes

Notes

Things to Remember

Important Dates

Books I want to Read

Movies I want to See

Places I want to Visit

Things that Inspire me

Events

Random Ideas

Year at a Glance

January
Sun	Mon	Tue	Wed	Thu	Fri	Sat

February
Sun	Mon	Tue	Wed	Thu	Fri	Sat

March
Sun	Mon	Tue	Wed	Thu	Fri	Sat

April
Sun	Mon	Tue	Wed	Thu	Fri	Sat

May
Sun	Mon	Tue	Wed	Thu	Fri	Sat

June
Sun	Mon	Tue	Wed	Thu	Fri	Sat

July
Sun	Mon	Tue	Wed	Thu	Fri	Sat

August
Sun	Mon	Tue	Wed	Thu	Fri	Sat

September
Sun	Mon	Tue	Wed	Thu	Fri	Sat

October
Sun	Mon	Tue	Wed	Thu	Fri	Sat

November
Sun	Mon	Tue	Wed	Thu	Fri	Sat

December
Sun	Mon	Tue	Wed	Thu	Fri	Sat

Week 1

Monday
DATE: __/__/__

Tuesday
DATE: __/__/__

Wednesday
DATE: __/__/__

> I'm grateful for the life I have

Thursday
DATE: __/__/__

Friday
DATE: __/__/__

Saturday
DATE: __/__/__

Sunday
DATE: __/__/__

Week 2

Monday
DATE: __/__/__

Tuesday
DATE: __/__/__

Wednesday
DATE: __/__/__

Today, I abandon my old habits and take up new, more positive ones

Thursday
DATE: __/__/__

Friday
DATE: __/__/__

Saturday
DATE: __/__/__

Sunday
DATE: __/__/__

Week 3

Monday
DATE: __/__/__

Tuesday
DATE: __/__/__

Wednesday
DATE: __/__/__

I can do this!

Thursday DATE: __/__/__

Friday DATE: __/__/__

Saturday DATE: __/__/__   # Sunday DATE: __/__/__

Week 4

Monday DATE: __/__/__

Tuesday DATE: __/__/__

Wednesday DATE: __/__/__

> I am honest in my life, and my work

Thursday DATE: __/__/__

Friday DATE: __/__/__

Saturday DATE: __/__/__   # Sunday DATE: __/__/__

Week 5

Monday
DATE: __/__/__

Tuesday
DATE: __/__/__

Wednesday
DATE: __/__/__

> Today, I am brimming with energy and overflowing with joy

Thursday
DATE: __/__/__

Friday
DATE: __/__/__

Saturday
DATE: __/__/__

Sunday
DATE: __/__/__

Week 6

Monday
DATE: __/__/__

Tuesday
DATE: __/__/__

Wednesday
DATE: __/__/__

> I have been given endless talents which I will begin to utilize today

Thursday
DATE: __/__/__

Friday
DATE: __/__/__

Saturday
DATE: __/__/__

Sunday
DATE: __/__/__

Week 7

Monday   date: __/__/__

Tuesday   date: __/__/__

Wednesday   date: __/__/__

> *I am excellent at what I do*

Thursday
DATE: _/_/_

Friday
DATE: _/_/_

Saturday
DATE: _/_/_

Sunday
DATE: _/_/_

Week 8

Monday
DATE: __/__/__

Tuesday
DATE: __/__/__

Wednesday
DATE: __/__/__

> I am the architect of my life; I build its foundation and choose its contents

Thursday DATE: __/__/__

Friday DATE: __/__/__

Saturday DATE: __/__/__

Sunday DATE: __/__/__

Week 9

Monday   DATE: __/__/__

Tuesday   DATE: __/__/__

Wednesday   DATE: __/__/__

> I forgive those who have harmed me in my past and peacefully detach from them

Thursday
DATE: __/__/__

Friday
DATE: __/__/__

Saturday
DATE: __/__/__

Sunday
DATE: __/__/__

Week 10

Monday
DATE: __/__/__

Tuesday
DATE: __/__/__

Wednesday
DATE: __/__/__

I am courageous and I stand up for myself

Thursday
DATE: __/__/__

Friday
DATE: __/__/__

Saturday
DATE: __/__/__

Sunday
DATE: __/__/__

Week 11

Monday   date: __/__/__

Tuesday   date: __/__/__

Wednesday   date: __/__/__

> I am a powerhouse; I am indestructible

Thursday
DATE: __/__/__

Friday
DATE: __/__/__

Saturday
DATE: __/__/__

Sunday
DATE: __/__/__

Week 12

Monday   date: __/__/__

Tuesday   date: __/__/__

Wednesday   date: __/__/__

> Though these times are difficult, they are only a short phase of life

Thursday date: _/_/_

Friday date: _/_/_

Saturday date: _/_/_   # Sunday date: _/_/_

Week 13

Monday DATE: __/__/__

Tuesday DATE: __/__/__

Wednesday DATE: __/__/__

My future is an ideal projection of what I envision now

Thursday DATE: _/_/_

Friday DATE: _/_/_

Saturday DATE: _/_/_   # Sunday DATE: _/_/_

Week 14

Monday   date: __/__/__

Tuesday   date: __/__/__

Wednesday   date: __/__/__

> I radiate beauty, charm, and grace

Thursday DATE: __/__/__

Friday DATE: __/__/__

Saturday DATE: __/__/__   # Sunday DATE: __/__/__

Week 15

Monday
DATE: __/__/__

Tuesday
DATE: __/__/__

Wednesday
DATE: __/__/__

> My obstacles are moving out of my way; my path is carved towards greatness

Thursday DATE: __/__/__

Friday DATE: __/__/__

Saturday DATE: __/__/__   # Sunday DATE: __/__/__

Week 16

Monday date: __/__/__

Tuesday date: __/__/__

Wednesday date: __/__/__

> *I wake up today with strength in my heart and clarity in my mind*

Thursday

DATE: __/__/__

Friday

DATE: __/__/__

Saturday

DATE: __/__/__

Sunday

DATE: __/__/__

Week 17

Monday DATE: __/__/__

Tuesday DATE: __/__/__

Wednesday DATE: __/__/__

> *My fears of tomorrow are simply melting away*

Thursday
DATE: __/__/__

Friday
DATE: __/__/__

Saturday
DATE: __/__/__

Sunday
DATE: __/__/__

Week 18

Monday Date: __/__/__

Tuesday Date: __/__/__

Wednesday Date: __/__/__

My life is just beginning

Thursday   date: __/__/__

Friday   date: __/__/__

Saturday   date: __/__/__   # Sunday   date: __/__/__

Week 19

Monday
DATE: __/__/__

Tuesday
DATE: __/__/__

Wednesday
DATE: __/__/__

I know, accept and am true to myself

Thursday DATE: __/__/__

Friday DATE: __/__/__

Saturday DATE: __/__/__   # Sunday DATE: __/__/__

Week 20

Monday   date: __/__/__

Tuesday   date: __/__/__

Wednesday   date: __/__/__

I learn from my mistakes

Thursday
DATE: __/__/__

Friday
DATE: __/__/__

Saturday
DATE: __/__/__

Sunday
DATE: __/__/__

Week 21

Monday
DATE: __/__/__

Tuesday
DATE: __/__/__

Wednesday
DATE: __/__/__

> *I forgive myself for not being perfect because I know I'm human*

Thursday DATE: _/_/_

Friday DATE: _/_/_

Saturday DATE: _/_/_   # Sunday DATE: _/_/_

Week 22

Monday   DATE: __/__/__

Tuesday   DATE: __/__/__

Wednesday   DATE: __/__/__

> I know I can accomplish anything I set my mind to

Thursday
DATE: __/__/__

Friday
DATE: __/__/__

Saturday
DATE: __/__/__

Sunday
DATE: __/__/__

Week 23

Monday
DATE: __/__/__

Tuesday
DATE: __/__/__

Wednesday
DATE: __/__/__

I never give up

Thursday DATE: __/__/__

Friday DATE: __/__/__

Saturday DATE: __/__/__   # Sunday DATE: __/__/__

Week 24

Monday DATE: __/__/__

Tuesday DATE: __/__/__

Wednesday DATE: __/__/__

> I am a unique and worthy person

Thursday

DATE: __/__/__

Friday

DATE: __/__/__

Saturday

DATE: __/__/__

Sunday

DATE: __/__/__

Week 25

Monday   date: __/__/__

Tuesday   date: __/__/__

Wednesday   date: __/__/__

> I accept what I cannot change

Thursday DATE: __/__/__

Friday DATE: __/__/__

Saturday DATE: __/__/__   # Sunday DATE: __/__/__

Week 26

Monday DATE: __/__/__

Tuesday DATE: __/__/__

Wednesday DATE: __/__/__

I make the best of every situation

Thursday DATE: __/__/__

Friday DATE: __/__/__

Saturday DATE: __/__/__   # Sunday DATE: __/__/__

Week 27

Monday   date: __/__/__

Tuesday   date: __/__/__

Wednesday   date: __/__/__

> I look for humor and fun in as many situations as possible

Thursday
DATE: __/__/__

Friday
DATE: __/__/__

Saturday
DATE: __/__/__

Sunday
DATE: __/__/__

Week 28

Monday   date: __/__/__

Tuesday   date: __/__/__

Wednesday   date: __/__/__

> *I turn obstacles into learning opportunities*

Thursday DATE: __/__/__

Friday DATE: __/__/__

Saturday DATE: __/__/__ # Sunday DATE: __/__/__

Week 29

Monday
DATE: __/__/__

Tuesday
DATE: __/__/__

Wednesday
DATE: __/__/__

> *I stand up for my beliefs, values and morals*

Thursday
DATE: __/__/__

Friday
DATE: __/__/__

Saturday
DATE: __/__/__

Sunday
DATE: __/__/__

Week 30

Monday
DATE: __/__/__

Tuesday
DATE: __/__/__

Wednesday
DATE: __/__/__

I treat others with respect and appreciate their individuality

Thursday
DATE: __/__/__

Friday
DATE: __/__/__

Saturday
DATE: __/__/__

Sunday
DATE: __/__/__

WEEK 31

MONDAY   DATE: __/__/__

TUESDAY   DATE: __/__/__

WEDNESDAY   DATE: __/__/__

> I contribute my talents and knowledge for the good of all

Thursday
DATE: __/__/__

Friday
DATE: __/__/__

Saturday
DATE: __/__/__

Sunday
DATE: __/__/__

Week 32

Monday   date: __/__/__

Tuesday   date: __/__/__

Wednesday   date: __/__/__

> *I make a difference whenever I can*

Thursday

DATE: __/__/__

Friday

DATE: __/__/__

Saturday

DATE: __/__/__

Sunday

DATE: __/__/__

Week 33

Monday
DATE: __/__/__

Tuesday
DATE: __/__/__

Wednesday
DATE: __/__/__

> I have a lot to offer

Thursday
DATE: __/__/__

Friday
DATE: __/__/__

Saturday
DATE: __/__/__

Sunday
DATE: __/__/__

Week 34

Monday
DATE: __/__/__

Tuesday
DATE: __/__/__

Wednesday
DATE: __/__/__

> I commit to learning new things

Thursday
DATE: __/__/__

Friday
DATE: __/__/__

Saturday
DATE: __/__/__

Sunday
DATE: __/__/__

Week 35

Monday
DATE: __/__/__

Tuesday
DATE: __/__/__

Wednesday
DATE: __/__/__

My thoughts are filled with positivity and my life is plentiful with prosperity

Thursday
DATE: __/__/__

Friday
DATE: __/__/__

Saturday
DATE: __/__/__

Sunday
DATE: __/__/__

Week 36

Monday
DATE: __/__/__

Tuesday
DATE: __/__/__

Wednesday
DATE: __/__/__

> I possess the qualities needed to be extremely successful

Thursday
DATE: __/__/__

Friday
DATE: __/__/__

Saturday
DATE: __/__/__

Sunday
DATE: __/__/__

Week 37

Monday
DATE: __/__/__

Tuesday
DATE: __/__/__

Wednesday
DATE: __/__/__

A river of compassion washes away my anger and replaces it with love

Thursday DATE: __/__/__

Friday DATE: __/__/__

Saturday DATE: __/__/__

Sunday DATE: __/__/__

Week 38

Monday   date: __/__/__

Tuesday   date: __/__/__

Wednesday   date: __/__/__

> *My ability to conquer my challenges is limitless; my potential to succeed is infinite*

Thursday DATE: __/__/__

....
....
....
....
....
....
....

Friday DATE: __/__/__

....
....
....
....
....
....
....

Saturday DATE: __/__/__   # Sunday DATE: __/__/__

Week 39

Monday DATE: __/__/__

Tuesday DATE: __/__/__

Wednesday DATE: __/__/__

> I am blessed with an incredible family and wonderful friends

Thursday DATE: __/__/__

Friday DATE: __/__/__

Saturday DATE: __/__/__ # Sunday DATE: __/__/__

Week 40

Monday   DATE: __/__/__

Tuesday   DATE: __/__/__

Wednesday   DATE: __/__/__

> I am at peace with all that has happened, is happening, and will happen

Thursday
DATE: __/__/__

Friday
DATE: __/__/__

Saturday
DATE: __/__/__

Sunday
DATE: __/__/__

Week 41

Monday DATE: __/__/__

Tuesday DATE: __/__/__

Wednesday DATE: __/__/__

I enjoy life to the fullest

Thursday DATE: _/_/__

Friday DATE: _/_/__

Saturday DATE: _/_/__ # Sunday DATE: _/_/__

Week 42

Monday DATE: __/__/__

Tuesday DATE: __/__/__

Wednesday DATE: __/__/__

> I accept others for who they are

Thursday   date: __/__/__

Friday   date: __/__/__

Saturday   date: __/__/__   # Sunday   date: __/__/__

Week 43

Monday DATE: __/__/__

Tuesday DATE: __/__/__

Wednesday DATE: __/__/__

I support and encourage others

Thursday
DATE: __/__/__

Friday
DATE: __/__/__

Saturday
DATE: __/__/__

Sunday
DATE: __/__/__

Week 44

Monday   date: __/__/__

Tuesday   date: __/__/__

Wednesday   date: __/__/__

> I live in the moment while learning from the past and preparing for the future

Thursday date: _/_/_

Friday date: _/_/_

Saturday date: _/_/_   # Sunday date: _/_/_

Week 45

Monday
DATE: __/__/__

Tuesday
DATE: __/__/__

Wednesday
DATE: __/__/__

I appreciate all the good things in my life

Thursday
DATE: __/__/__

Friday
DATE: __/__/__

Saturday
DATE: __/__/__

Sunday
DATE: __/__/__

WEEK 46

MONDAY   DATE: __/__/__

TUESDAY   DATE: __/__/__

WEDNESDAY   DATE: __/__/__

> I believe everything works out for the best

Thursday DATE: __/__/__

Friday DATE: __/__/__

Saturday DATE: __/__/__   # Sunday DATE: __/__/__

Week 47

Monday   DATE: __/__/__

Tuesday   DATE: __/__/__

Wednesday   DATE: __/__/__

> I aspire to live a life that has meaning to me

Thursday
DATE: __/__/__

Friday
DATE: __/__/__

Saturday
DATE: __/__/__

Sunday
DATE: __/__/__

Week 48

Monday date: __/__/__

Tuesday date: __/__/__

Wednesday date: __/__/__

Nothing can dim the light that shines from within

Thursday DATE: __/__/__

Friday DATE: __/__/__

Saturday DATE: __/__/__ # Sunday DATE: __/__/__

Week 49

Monday   date: __/__/__

Tuesday   date: __/__/__

Wednesday   date: __/__/__

I allow myself to be who I am without judgment

Thursday DATE: _/_/_

Friday DATE: _/_/_

Saturday DATE: _/_/_ # Sunday DATE: _/_/_

Week 50

Monday
DATE: __/__/__

Tuesday
DATE: __/__/__

Wednesday
DATE: __/__/__

I listen to my intuition and trust my inner guide

Thursday DATE: __/__/__

Friday DATE: __/__/__

Saturday DATE: __/__/__

Sunday DATE: __/__/__

Week 51

Monday
DATE: __/__/__

Tuesday
DATE: __/__/__

Wednesday
DATE: __/__/__

> I accept my emotions and let them serve their purpose

Thursday DATE: _/_/_

Friday DATE: _/_/_

Saturday DATE: _/_/_ # Sunday DATE: _/_/_

Week 52

Monday
DATE: __/__/__

Tuesday
DATE: __/__/__

Wednesday
DATE: __/__/__

> I am loved, loving and lovable

Thursday
DATE: __/__/__

Friday
DATE: __/__/__

Saturday
DATE: __/__/__

Sunday
DATE: __/__/__

Week 53

Monday   DATE: __/__/__

Tuesday   DATE: __/__/__

Wednesday   DATE: __/__/__

> *I give out love and it is returned to me multiplied manyfold*

Thursday DATE: __/__/__

Friday DATE: __/__/__

Saturday DATE: __/__/__ # Sunday DATE: __/__/__

Notes

Notes

> I forgive myself and set myself free

Notes

Notes

Notes

Notes

> I am full of positive loving energy

Notes

Notes

Notes

Notes

> *I make a difference in the world by simply existing in it*

Notes

Notes

Notes

Notes

> I am worthy of my dreams

Notes

Notes

Notes

Notes

I am enough

Notes

Notes

Notes

Notes

Notes

Notes

NOTES

NOTES

Notes

Notes

Notes

Notes

Copyright © 2021 Susan McKenzie

ISBN: 978-1-922413-01-7

All rights reserved, including the right to reproduce this book, or portions thereof, in any form. No part of this text may be reproduced, transmitted, downloaded, decompiled, reverse engineered, or stored in or introduced into any information storage and retrieval system, in any form or by any means, whether electronic or mechanical without the express written permission of the author. The scanning, uploading, and distribution of this book via the Internet or via any other means without the permission of the author is illegal and punishable by law. Please purchase only authorised electronic or paperback editions, and do not participate in or encourage electronic piracy of copyrighted materials.

Cover art © 2021 Susan McKenzie

Amazon author page: amazon.com/author/susancarter

Visit the author's website: http://susanmckenzieauthor.com

Follow Sue on Twitter: https://twitter.com/SusanMcKenzie68

Follow Sue on Facebook: https://www.facebook.com/SueMcKenzieAuthor

Graphics used in this book are attributed to:
Starline/Freepik
Kjpargeter/Freepik
Alvaro_Cabrera/Freepik
www.freepngimg.com
www.kindpng.com

www.ingramcontent.com/pod-product-compliance
Lightning Source LLC
Chambersburg PA
CBHW081336080526
44588CB00017B/2642